W9-DDM-016

TV DISPLAYS DISASTER AS THE
CHALLENGER EXPLODES

An Augmented Reading Experience

By Rebecca Rissman

Content Adviser: Alan Schroeder, Professor,
School of Journalism, Northeastern University

COMPASS POINT BOOKS
a capstone imprint

Compass Point Books are published by Capstone Press,
1710 Roe Crest Drive, North Mankato, Minnesota 56003
www.capstonepub.com

Editorial Credits
Michelle Bisson, editor; Tracy McCabe, designer; Svetlana Zhurkin, media researcher;
Katy LaVigne, production specialist

Photo Credits
AP Photo, 36; Getty Images: Bettmann, 19; Library of Congress, 57 (top); NASA, cover, 5, 6, 7, 9, 13, 15, 17, 21, 22, 23, 28, 29, 31, 41, 45, 46, 47, 49, 53, 56, 57 (bottom), 58, 59, Bill Bowers, 11, Bill Ingalls, 54, Otis Imboden, 26; Newscom: Everett Collection, 33, United Archives/IFA Film, 24, Zuma Press/Michael Evans, 43; Science Source: NASA, 34

Library of Congress Cataloging-in-Publication Data
Names: Rissman, Rebecca, author.

Title: TV displays disaster as the Challenger explodes : 4D, an augmented reading experience / by Rebecca Rissman.
Description: North Mankato, Minnesota : Compass Point Books, [2020] | Series: Captured television history 4D
Identifiers: LCCN 2019002576| ISBN 9780756559984 (hardcover) | ISBN 9780756560027 (pbk.) | ISBN 9780756560065 (ebook PDF)
Subjects: LCSH: Challenger (Spacecraft)—Accidents—Juvenile literature. | Space vehicle accidents—United States—Juvenile literature. | Television broadcasting of news—United States—Juvenile literature.
Classification: LCC TL867 .R57 2020 | DDC 363.12/4—dc23
LC record available at https://lccn.loc.gov/2019002576

All internet sites appearing in the back matter were available and accurate when this book was sent to press.

Download the Capstone app!

- Ask an adult to download the Capstone 4D app.

- Scan the cover and stars inside the book for additional content.

When you scan a spread, you'll find fun extra stuff to go with this book! You can also find these things on the web at www.capstone4D.com using the password: challenger.59984

Printed and bound in the United States of America.
PA70

TABLEOFCONTENTS

ChapterOne
GO FOR LAUNCH

It was just before 8:00 a.m. on January 28, 1986. A crew of seven astronauts stepped out of a National Aeronautics and Space Administration (NASA) facility and into a crisp, frigid Florida morning. The astronauts wore light blue jumpsuits. They smiled brightly. A crowd of fans and reporters cheered excitedly. The mood was optimistic. After five days of delays, it looked as though NASA's next space shuttle mission, STS-51L, would finally launch. A NASA publicist shouted to the crew, "Looks like we're going this morning." Christa McAuliffe, one of the astronauts, turned and gave her joyful reply: "Great."

Television news crews filmed the astronauts as they boarded a long, silver NASA bus and departed. They were heading about 3 miles (5 kilometers) away to Launch Complex 39. There, towering above Pad B, they found their spacecraft: a black and white orbiter called Challenger. It hung between two 149-foot- (45-meter-) tall solid rocket boosters and piggybacked the 154-foot- (47-m-) tall external tank. But the crew also found something else on the launchpad: ice. It was clinging to many structures at the pad. Icicles hung in long, dripping clusters from pipes. Sheets of ice coated metal walkways. It was the coldest launch morning in NASA's history.

The crew of Challenger started their fateful mission on a freezing cold January day.

Icicles clung to the launchpad despite the ice crew's efforts to remove them.

Ice crews had worked during the night to remove as much ice as possible from launch structures. But now, as launch approached, some wondered if they had done enough. Ice could be very dangerous during a launch. An icicle could break off and puncture a rocket or damage the orbiter. Or a chunk of ice could get sucked up into one of the orbiter's powerful engines. This could cause an explosion. Launching on such a cold morning might be a dangerous move.

Christa McAuliffe was selected as the first Teacher in Space. Her participation drew wide public attention to the space program.

The astronauts took an elevator to the crew level of Challenger. When the doors opened, they made their way across a small walkway to the white room. This would be their final stop before entering their spacecraft and home for the next seven days. As they walked, a NASA tech stopped McAuliffe. He handed her an apple. This was a symbol of her role on the flight. McAuliffe was to be the first participant in NASA's Teacher in Space project. Happily, McAuliffe smiled and said, "Save it for me and I'll eat it when I get back."

Inside the white room, techs in white suits helped the crew put on their space helmets and padded flight vests. Then they carefully crawled into Challenger.

Dick Scobee, the mission's commander, climbed onto the shuttle's flight deck. This was the section of the space shuttle that contained the cockpit. It housed all the flight controls. Its blue-gray walls and ceiling were crowded with instruments, screens, and buttons. Six small windows curved along the front of the cockpit. These promised to give the crew a glimpse of the stars.

Scobee slid into the most important spot in the spacecraft: the front left seat. Scobee was a retired Air Force pilot, experimental test pilot, and experienced astronaut. Scobee had flown in space once before as pilot on board STS-41C in 1984. That mission had also taken place on board the orbiter Challenger. Next to Scobee, Michael J. Smith buckled himself into the pilot's seat. Smith was a Navy commander and former test pilot. This would be his first space mission. Just behind Scobee and Smith, engineer and astronaut Judy Resnik climbed into her seat. This would be Resnik's second spaceflight. She had flown on board STS-41D in 1984. Resnik was a mission specialist. This meant that she worked alongside the pilot and commander to maintain the orbiter. She would also launch satellites and do scientific experiments. To Resnik's right, another

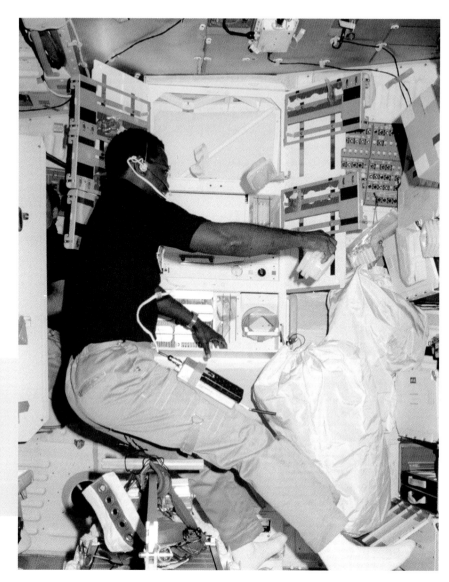

mission specialist, named Ellison S. Onizuka, buckled himself in and prepared for liftoff. Onizuka had flown in space once before, on STS-51C in 1985.

Just below the flight deck, three more astronauts settled into the middeck. This area held crew equipment and electronics as well as three flight seats. Mission specialist Ronald McNair strapped himself into the far rear seat. McNair was a physicist and astronaut. He had flown on board STS-41B as a mission specialist. That mission had also taken place on board Challenger. The two remaining seats were filled by two payload specialists. Their job on Challenger was to conduct experiments or research in space. One was former Air Force pilot and engineer Greg Jarvis. He planned to do research on the mission that would help the development of liquid-fueled rockets. The last seat was filled by schoolteacher Christa McAuliffe. She planned to teach two live lessons to children from the space shuttle. They would air on the television station PBS. McAuliffe would also film six other lessons. These would be distributed after the mission.

Once the full crew was loaded into the orbiter, support technicians helped ensure that everything was ready for launch. They double-checked that each astronaut's radio worked. They adjusted the temperature inside the orbiter. The astronauts nervously joked with one another. Launch was scheduled to occur just after 9:30 a.m.

Then Ground Control messaged the crew: It was still below freezing. NASA policy stated that launch could not occur until the outside temperatures rose to at least 31 degrees Fahrenheit (minus 0.6 degrees Celsius). This rise in temperature would help some of the ice on the launchpad melt. It would also warm the rockets and make the launch safer for the crew.

Before the flight, astronauts rehearsed their launch positions and roles.

Three miles (5 km) away, small crowds gathered to watch the launch from viewing areas. Journalists and fans stood in the bright sunshine, bundled against the biting cold. Camera operators set up video cameras in front of McAuliffe's family. They hoped to capture their excited reactions to the launch on film. Photographers snapped photo after photo.

The clock ticked past 10:00 a.m. The temperatures were rising. This was good for the crew of Challenger. It looked as if they might just fly. It was a bit after 11:00 a.m., and the temperature was now 36°F (2.2°C).

Launch Control told the crew that they should prepare to move forward with their countdown toward launch.

Mission Specialist Resnik was delighted. She responded, "Aaall riight!"

In school auditoriums, gyms, and classrooms around the country, millions of American schoolchildren prepared to watch the launch on television. McAuliffe's role on the flight had made this mission especially exciting for the children. Students eagerly waited to watch a teacher launch. Educators, too, looked forward to seeing STS-51L begin on television. It would be thrilling to watch one of their own become a space traveler. Many Florida teachers ushered their children outside so that they could see the shuttle soar through the blue sky.

As launch grew nearer, one Florida teacher shushed her class: "Be quiet, history [is] being made by a teacher."

The crew spent the last few minutes before launch busily getting ready. They locked their helmet visors in place and tightened their seat restraints. At T-minus seven minutes, giant support structures began to pull away from the spacecraft assembly in preparation for launch.

At T-minus 52 seconds, a routine cabin alarm sounded. Everything looked good.

"Thirty seconds down there," Commander Scobee announced into his headset microphone. It was almost time. ". . . Fifteen."

TEACHER IN SPACE PROJECT

(Left to right): Gregory Jarvis helped train Christa McAuliffe and Barbara Morgan in the Teacher in Space Project. Morgan flew on a shuttle mission in 1998.

In 1984 President Ronald Reagan introduced NASA's Teacher in Space Project. It would allow a citizen schoolteacher to become an astronaut. This was a big change for NASA. Previous astronauts had come from engineering, scientific, or aviation backgrounds. Many were from the military. Reagan thought that allowing a teacher to be an astronaut would make space seem more relatable to the country. He also said that it would remind Americans of the "crucial role that teachers and education play in the life of our nation." Many at NASA hoped that the Teacher in Space Project would make Americans more enthusiastic about space.

More than 11,000 teachers applied to become astronauts. In June 1985 NASA chose 114 semifinalists. These were narrowed down to only 10. These candidates were sent to the Johnson Space Center in Houston, Texas. There, they underwent a series of rigorous tests to determine their ability to withstand the stresses of spaceflight. The teachers' blood, urine, heart, and lungs were tested. They ran on treadmills and allowed themselves to be zipped into fitted black bags in order to test their response to claustrophobia. They underwent psychiatric interviews and experienced brief moments of weightlessness on special airplane flights to test their response to motion sickness.

Finally on July 19, 1985, Vice President George H.W. Bush announced the winner: Sharon Christa McAuliffe. She was a New Hampshire high school teacher whose classes focused on social studies, economics, history, and law.

McAuliffe appeared on several TV shows, including *The Today Show, The Tonight Show,* and *Good Morning America.* Her enthusiastic, friendly personality made her a popular public figure. This was a big success for NASA. McAuliffe was drawing attention to the space program in a positive way.

Schoolchildren watching the launch cheered excitedly. Many joined in on the countdown, chanting along with the voice broadcast over the television.

At T-minus six seconds, the crew felt their engines rumble to life. "There they go, guys," Commander Scobee exclaimed.

"All right!" Resnik whooped.

At 11:38 a.m. the orbiter's three main engines erupted with full force. "Here we go," said pilot Smith.

Challenger's huge engines roared with power. Giant plumes of white smoke billowed around the launchpad. The space shuttle heaved into the air. From the distant viewing platforms, everything about the launch looked great.

As Challenger soared, it encountered strong winds. They shook the crew inside. Nineteen seconds after launch, Smith noted, "Looks like we've got a lotta wind here today." Commander Scobee agreed, "Yeah. It's a little hard to see out my window here."

At 40 seconds, Smith said, "There's Mach 1." They had broken the sound barrier. The shuttle continued to climb. At 19,000 feet (5,791 m), it reduced speed briefly. This change in speed helped it travel safely through the Max Q. This was a short and planned reduction in speed. After just 14 seconds, Commander Scobee announced that he was throttling back up. The shuttle began accelerating.

At first, the Challenger launch seemed to go well.

At one minute and two seconds, Smith noted their altitude and speed: 35,000 feet (10,668 m) and Mach 1.5. Everything seemed to be going well for the crew. This was good. It was incredibly difficult for shuttle crews to abort their missions in the very early stages of liftoff.

On the ground, photographers worked to keep Challenger in their view. It soared across the blue sky, leaving a puffy white contrail in its wake. Fans—crowded onto viewing platforms—cheered and clapped. The McAuliffe family embraced happily.

A few local news crews filmed the launch. Their footage would be played during their news broadcasts later in the day. NASA cameras were also there. They captured the launch. Crews then sent their footage via satellite to schools around the country. This allowed many millions of American children to watch the launch live from their schools. Only one national TV network, CNN, broadcast the event live. Compared to earlier launches, this was a very small turnout of television news crews. But still, the mood was happy and excited among those present.

On board Challenger, Commander Scobee and pilot Smith were busy updating ground crews on their progress. They rattled off their speed into their radios. As far as they were concerned, the mission was going perfectly well. Then something strange happened.

One minute and 13 seconds after launch, Smith uttered an unusual phrase into his microphone: "Uh oh."

On the ground, viewers watched as Challenger suddenly disappeared behind a burst of white smoke. Orange flames flickered inside the billowing cloud. The solid rocket boosters shot wildly away, leaving two thick, white contrails snaking behind. More streaks of white rocketed away from the cloud, creating an enormous, drooping lightning bolt of smoke in the sky.

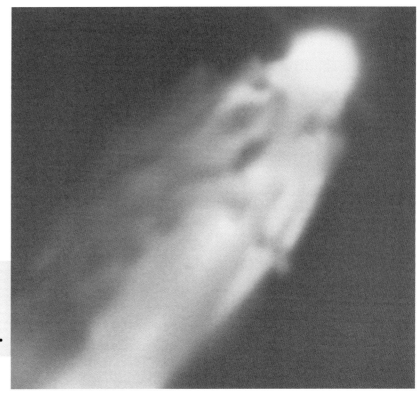

Slightly more than a minute into the flight, Challenger seemed to disappear.

Cameras on the ground captured the reactions of people on the viewing platforms. At first, they looked confused. Some exchanged puzzled glances. Others squinted into the sky, searching for a glimpse of the shuttle amid the smoke. Some cried out in shock.

Schoolchildren watching the launch fell quiet. Their teachers wondered what had happened. They didn't know what to say to their students.

NASA's commentator, Steve Nesbitt, added to the confusion. His voice was broadcast over NASA's public address system. Nesbitt had been rattling off numbers during the launch. He was so focused on his job of reporting on the launch status numbers from his computer that he was not looking at the actual launch. After the cloud erupted in the sky, Nesbitt continued reading his figures aloud: "One minute fifteen seconds, velocity 2,900 feet per second. Altitude nine nautical miles. Range distance seven nautical miles."

It was only after someone in Mission Control got Nesbitt's attention that he looked up and saw what had happened. He fell silent. NASA officials inside Mission Control scrambled to figure it out. Some wondered if the orbiter had survived whatever had occurred in the sky. People on the launch viewing platforms asked one another, "Where's the shuttle? Where's the shuttle?"

Nesbitt spoke again. "Flight controllers here are looking very carefully at the situation. Obviously a major malfunction. . . . We have the report from the flight dynamics officer that the vehicle has exploded."

News cameras captured the shocked reactions of the people standing on the viewing platforms. Some cried. Others stared—dumbfounded—into the sky. They had just witnessed the worst disaster in the history of the U.S. space program.

When Challenger launched, a relatively small number of Americans were watching. But by the end of the day, many millions would watch the video footage over and over. Television news networks interrupted regular broadcasts to alert their viewers to the disaster. Clips of the explosion were aired on evening news programs. In this way, television

"We have the report from the flight dynamics officer that the vehicle has exploded."

brought the Challenger disaster into living rooms and classrooms across the nation. It also transformed a momentary explosion into a tragedy that stretched across hours, days, weeks, months, and years. Even today, footage of the Challenger disaster remains a powerful reminder of both the dangers of spaceflight and the incredible reach of television.

ChapterTwo
THE SPACE SHUTTLE PROGRAM

When Challenger launched on that cold January morning in 1986, many Americans had grown bored with NASA and its giant space shuttles. After all, the space shuttle program, also known as the Space Transportation System (STS), had been around since the early 1970s. Mission STS-51L was NASA's 25th shuttle launch. This made it appear as though U.S. spaceflight had become routine.

Exploring outer space had not always seemed dull. In its early days, NASA's space launches were thrilling affairs. Americans clamored to watch the country's first astronauts climb into their tiny capsules and blast into space. Approximately 135 million people watched astronaut John Glenn as he orbited Earth on February 20, 1962. This was the largest yet recorded television audience in history. These pioneering missions were celebrations of American industry and innovation. Television news networks went to great lengths to inform and entertain their viewers as the astronauts launched, flew, and landed. Even after their missions had ended, the astronauts remained celebrated heroes. They gave television interviews. They were also treated to parades, parties, and visits to meet the president at the White House.

John Glenn became famous as the first American to orbit Earth. He later served as a congressman.

The early days of the space shuttle had been exciting too. Unlike the small space capsules used in the past, the shuttle was very large. It was about the same size and shape as a midsized airliner. It landed on a runway, much like an airplane. Another thing that made it unique was that much of the STS was reusable. The orbiter and solid rocket boosters were meant to be used over and over. This would save NASA—and the federal budget—a lot of money. But more than the cost-saving aspects and updated design, the shuttle was exciting because it represented a new phase of American spaceflight.

The space shuttle would allow astronauts and astronaut-scientists to spend more time in space than before. They could travel in larger crews. The orbiter's cargo bay also allowed them to take large pieces of equipment, such as satellites, into space.

In 1976 NASA unveiled its first model of the shuttle. It was called Enterprise. NASA flew and tested Enterprise within Earth's atmosphere to make

Guion "Guy" Bluford Jr. was the first African American man in space.

sure that it was safe for spaceflight. Then on April 12, 1981, NASA launched its first operational shuttle into space. It was called Columbia. Much as they had during NASA's first spaceflights, journalists and fans flocked to Florida to watch the launch. The event was broadcast live around the U.S. and in several European countries. Columbia remained in space for two days before returning to Earth. When Columbia landed on April 14, more than 150,000 people gathered to watch and cheer. Millions more watched on TV.

Some subsequent shuttle flights continued to interest the U.S. public. In June 1983 Sally Ride became the first American woman to fly in space on board Challenger. Two months later, Guion "Guy" Bluford Jr. became the first African American man in space on another Challenger mission. These momentous firsts kept the public engaged with the shuttle program.

TELEVISION, *STAR TREK*, AND THE SPACE SHUTTLE ENTERPRISE

Enterprise was named after the spaceship featured in the TV drama Star Trek.

In the early years of the space shuttle program, television was influenced by the country's renewed interest in space travel. Popular TV dramas such as *Star Trek* occasionally referenced NASA's accomplishments in its plots. In turn, NASA was also influenced by the country's interest in *Star Trek*. The first space shuttle was intended to be named the Constitution. However, *Star Trek* fans had something else in mind. They organized a letter-writing campaign to the White House. Hundreds of thousands of letters poured in requesting that the shuttle instead be named Enterprise, after a *Star Trek* spaceship.

NASA officials likely knew that appealing to public interests would help make their shuttle program more popular. Many people at the White House agreed. Naming the ship Enterprise would also recall the diverse, egalitarian society featured in the show. This could appeal to a nation that was becoming more diverse.

On September 17, 1976, NASA unveiled its model space shuttle to a crowd of thousands. It was named Enterprise. To mark the occasion, many *Star Trek* cast members appeared at the unveiling.

As the years went on, the sense of fun and excitement around shuttle flights began to fade. The public gradually lost interest. Part of this had to do with the frequency of shuttle missions. By January 1986, the first operational shuttle, Columbia, had flown in space seven times. Subsequent shuttles kept up this pace. Discovery had flown six missions. Atlantis had flown two. And Challenger, the busiest of the orbiters, had flown nine successful missions. This meant that in a period of just 57 months, NASA successfully facilitated 24 shuttle missions.

The frequency of shuttle missions was not the only reason for the dwindling public interest. Many Americans had also begun to think of spaceflight as an elite, scientific, and somewhat boring activity. This made it hard for many people to relate to. Also, people began to think of spaceflight as a very safe endeavor. Only three Americans had ever died in a NASA spacecraft accident. Back in 1967, astronauts Gus Grissom, Ed White, and Roger Chaffee had died during a preflight test in an Apollo capsule. In the years following this accident, NASA had gone to great lengths to improve safety protocols. It had also learned much more about spaceflight and engineering.

Over time, television news networks reduced shuttle launch coverage. This saved the networks money. Sending reporters and cameras to Cape Canaveral, Florida, could be very expensive. And with

After many successful space missions, shuttle launches became routine and attracted only fierce fans.

fewer Americans interested in following launches, it did not make sense for networks to invest in coverage.

On the morning of Challenger's launch, a small number of journalists were in Cape Canaveral to report on the mission. Only one major news network, CNN, planned to show the launch live. NASA had hoped that the presence of the first schoolteacher in space would boost interest in the mission. Christa McAuliffe's bubbly, warm personality had, indeed, engaged the public. However, compared to NASA's first spaceflights, the Challenger mission seemed relatively unimportant. In addition, a major space story had just occurred four days prior to the launch. A space probe called Voyager 2 had done a flyby of Uranus. Many science and space journalists were still focused on that story. Finally, the weather in

Cape Canaveral was extremely cold. Many members of the press assumed that the shuttle launch would be delayed. Therefore, they hadn't traveled there to watch.

Many news outlets that did not send crews to Cape Canaveral still planned to make the launch into a special segment for their evening news. Some networks filmed local schoolteachers and their classrooms watching the launch. Others filmed backup footage of the launch complex early that morning to add to broadcasts they would air later in the day. For example, CBS News did not plan to show the launch live. However, the network still sent a reporter and camera to film footage to use later. This choice showed that CBS did not think the launch would be very important.

Though Challenger didn't get much attention from news networks, it remained an exciting event for schoolchildren and teachers. Millions of American children looked forward to watching the nation's first teacher fly into space. Educators, too, felt a connection with McAuliffe. They wanted to share her accomplishment with their students.

Many schools turned to CNN to allow their students to watch the launch live. Others chose NASA TV. This was a NASA-owned television service. It provided live coverage for educators. It also allowed other television outlets to access its video. This meant that television news organizations that did not send their own camera operators to the launch could utilize NASA's footage for their own broadcasts.

A CBS news crew videotaped students at McAuliffe's Concord, New Hampshire, school as they watched the launch in an auditorium. When Challenger lifted away from the launchpad, the students cheered and threw streamers into the air. It was a thrilling moment for the American spaceflight program, and for American schoolchildren as well.

"Space expenditures must take their proper place within a rigorous system of national priorities."

External Tank

Solid Rocket Booster

Solid Rocket Booster

Orbiter

USA

NASA Challenger

SAVING MONEY WITH THE SPACE SHUTTLE

Space shuttles were more economical than other spaceships because shuttles could be reused.

Though the huge shuttles and their towering rockets looked impressive, they were actually created out of the need to save money. NASA's early space missions had been incredibly expensive. They had been wasteful too. The Mercury, Gemini, and Apollo capsules could be flown only once. The rockets used to propel them into space were also single-use. This meant that each one of NASA's early missions cost the American public a lot of money.

President Richard Nixon valued NASA's work, but he thought the space program was taking too much money from the American public. In 1966 NASA's budget had taken up $5.9 billion of the federal budget. Nixon reduced it to $4.25 billion in 1969. He said, "Space expenditures must take their proper place within a rigorous system of national priorities." In 1970 Nixon urged NASA to "devise less costly and less complicated ways of transporting payloads into space."

On January 5, 1972, Nixon signed a bill that allocated $5.5 billion to the development of the shuttle. He hoped that this would usher in a new phase of safe, frequent American spaceflight.

ChapterThree
CHALLENGER DISASTER

At just after 11:30 a.m., three newscasters at CNN prepared their audience for Challenger's launch. Tom Mintier appeared on camera and cheerfully announced, "The ice has cleared away and Challenger should be going away very soon."

CNN then switched to video of the space shuttle on the launchpad. As viewers watched, support arms holding the shuttle to the launch structure began to peel away slowly. Over the video, CNN played NASA's live radio communication. This included the voice of Hugh Harris from Launch Control. He steadily read off important updates. He also marked the countdown. As launch neared, CNN showed different views of the shuttle. Some long-distance shots showed how enormous the launch complex was. Others were zoomed-in shots of the rocket engines. These emphasized the power that was about to erupt.

While Harris counted down the last seconds toward the launch, CNN showed a close-up of the orbiter's powerful main engines as they burst to life. Orange flames shot downward. Harris said, "We have main engines start. Four, three, two, one, and liftoff! Liftoff of the 25th space shuttle mission and it has cleared the tower!" Challenger lurched away from the ground.

As Challenger exploded, fragments of the orbiter could be seen against the background of fire, smoke, and vapor.

A nearly imperceptible puff of gray smoke shot out from the side of one of the solid rocket boosters.

The shuttle began to streak into the sky. NASA's radio communications between the ground and shuttle crews were piped into the televised footage. Commander Scobee announced, "Houston, Challenger roll program." A ground crew member responded, "Roger roll, Challenger." This acknowledged that the shuttle and rockets were falling into their proper position. News cameras captured this action. The big, brown external tank rotated upwards. The orbiter rolled into the lower position.

Video camera operators on the ground worked hard to keep Challenger in their frames as it shot up into the deepening blue sky. A giant trail of fire followed. CNN viewers listened to launch updates from Steve Nesbitt. He listed off numbers related to the engines, fuel, and throttle. Behind his voice was the muffled roar of the shuttle's engines. As the shuttle blazed upward, the video quality began to degrade. The picture became grainier and shakier as camera operators zoomed in on the shrinking spacecraft.

As the shuttle rose toward space, it encountered violent winds. These buffeted, or rocked, the spacecraft. Challenger's computer system worked to adjust to the turbulent conditions. These winds,

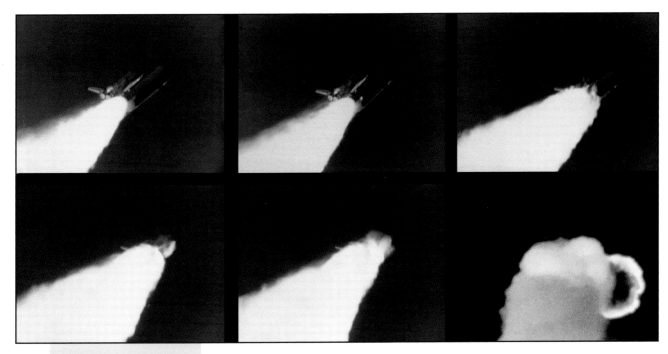

These six images show the stages of the Challenger flight and explosion from 58.8 to 109.6 seconds after launch.

combined with the stresses of Max Q, strained the spacecraft. But Challenger was designed to withstand intense forces and still survive.

There was, however, one element of the launch that Challenger could not survive. The morning's freezing temperatures had affected components inside the solid rocket boosters called O-rings. These rubber rings worked to seal the rocket's various fuel compartments. The morning's extreme cold caused the O-rings to become brittle. As the shuttle blasted off, one set of O-rings failed. This allowed a puff of very hot exhaust to leak out from the side of the rocket. This changed the temperature of the rocket's exterior. It made the rocket extremely unstable. What had begun as a small puff of smoke would soon become a huge explosion.

COLD WEATHER AND O-RINGS

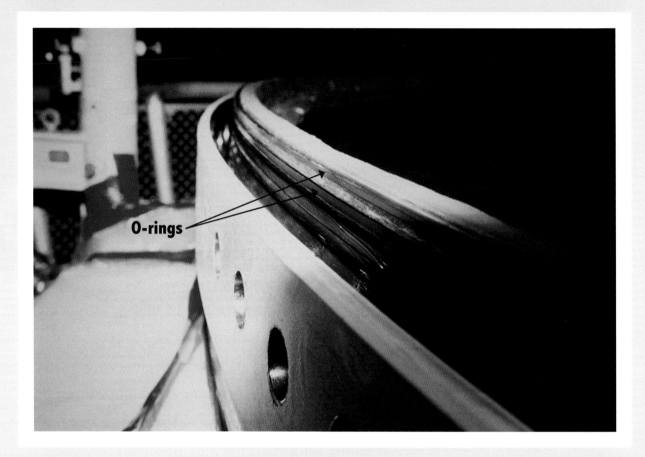

O-rings

The O-rings that failed are visible below the yellow putty on top of the rocket booster.

NASA had hired a company called Morton Thiokol to build the shuttle's solid rocket boosters. Engineers at Morton Thiokol knew that low temperatures affected the solid rocket boosters' O-rings. They understood that cold weather could make the launches very dangerous. Morton Thiokol even issued a general warning: NASA should not launch a shuttle in temperatures colder than 53°F (12°C).

On January 27, 1986, the night before the Challenger disaster, the engineers at Morton Thiokol advised their managers that the temperatures were much too low for a launch. The managers then passed this warning on to NASA. People at the space agency were not happy. One said, "I am appalled . . ." Another said, "My God. . . . When do you want [us] to launch—next April?" NASA pressured Morton Thiokol to prove that the shuttle could not fly in such cold weather. Under this pressure, the management at Morton Thiokol gave in. They decided that Challenger was "Go" for launch.

Morton Thiokol engineers feared that if an O-ring failed, the shuttle would explode on the launchpad. When Challenger heaved off the ground, engineers watching the launch were relieved. One engineer remembers a colleague excitedly shouting, "We made it! We made it!" But just a few seconds later, they realized that their prediction had come true.

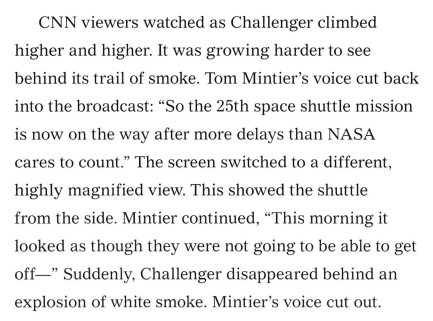

"Looks like a couple of the solid rocket boosters blew away from the side of the shuttle in an explosion."

CNN viewers watched as Challenger climbed higher and higher. It was growing harder to see behind its trail of smoke. Tom Mintier's voice cut back into the broadcast: "So the 25th space shuttle mission is now on the way after more delays than NASA cares to count." The screen switched to a different, highly magnified view. This showed the shuttle from the side. Mintier continued, "This morning it looked as though they were not going to be able to get off—" Suddenly, Challenger disappeared behind an explosion of white smoke. Mintier's voice cut out.

The screen switched to a wide shot. This showed a growing cloud of smoke in the air. NASA's Steve Nesbitt continued rattling off his technical updates. Mintier was silent. After a few seconds, the shaken newscaster said, "Looks like a couple of the solid rocket boosters blew away from the side of the shuttle in an explosion. . . ."

As Mintier struggled to communicate what he had just watched, reporters in Cape Canaveral, Florida, erupted into a frenzy. They ran from their viewing site into the Kennedy Center's public affairs building, hoping to get some information on what had occurred. CNN News correspondent John Zarrella was among the crowd. He later said it was a moment of "total chaos," with "reporters screaming at NASA," and the agency's public information officers "screaming back at the reporters."

Suddenly, what had seemed like a boring, unimportant launch was urgent news.

In schoolrooms across the nation, children struggled to understand what they had just seen on television. Students at Christa McAuliffe's Concord, New Hampshire, school sat in dumbfounded silence. They stared at the screen at the front of the auditorium in shock. Adults at the back of the room quietly embraced. Teachers and students alike waited for updates from the news. What had just happened? Was the crew okay?

"... it's a breaking story, obviously an important story ... the kind of news that nobody wants to report."

News producers at CNN hurried to find answers. The newsroom behind Tom Mintier burst into action. Producers scrambled to organize their news crews in Florida. They rushed to look through their informational packets on the space shuttles, trying to understand what might have happened. The noise level in the newsroom rose. It was a frantic environment. Producers and writers were having a hard time hearing one another. At one point, a man in the newsroom actually stood up and shouted, "Shut up in here!"

CNN was not alone in its chaotic efforts to report on the event. Minutes after the shuttle disappeared in the sky, other cable news networks began to pick up the story. At 11:42 a.m. NBC broke into its national programming to report on the disaster. ABC followed one minute later. CBS was next at 11:45 a.m.

Dan Rather handled the story at CBS. After playing footage of the explosion, Rather said, "This story is in the—it's a breaking story, obviously an important story, a big story, the kind of news that nobody wants to report." CBS soon switched from video of Rather at his desk to a shot of the now-empty launchpad. Smoke still clung to its structures.

Rather's reporting showed just how little anyone knew in the moments after the launch. He repeatedly announced that something had happened to the shuttle. But he reminded his viewers that the fate of the crew was still unknown. At one point, Rather even admitted, "What you have here is you have a reporter who is vamping for time at the moment because we hope to get more information as we are on the air."

Viewers tuning in to ABC and NBC saw similar coverage. Newscasters listened intently to their earpiece radios for any updates from their producers. Then they did their best to communicate this information to their audiences. News producers cut between footage of the explosion, Mission Control in Houston, the launchpad in Florida, and their own newsrooms.

In 1986, CNN was the only network that aired news 24 hours each day. Other outlets, such as CBS, NBC, and ABC, occasionally extended their newscasts to cover significant events. For example, in 1969, CBS devoted a full 31 hours to broadcasting the moon landing. However, this was an exception. Producers had plenty of time to plan for the moon landing broadcast. They supplemented their video with animation, guests, and other special features. When newscasters dropped everything to devote hours to the Challenger disaster, their presentations were often choppy and rough.

Adding to the rough nature of the newscasts was the lack of information from NASA. The space agency was nearly overwhelmed by the hectic

"What you have here is you have a reporter who is vamping for time at the moment . . ."

response to the explosion. The agency's phone system became overloaded with the volume of calls. In fact, shortly after the disaster, the telephone system for the surrounding area in Florida, including Orlando, was entirely lost for several hours. NASA was forced to rely on an intercom system and walkie-talkies to communicate with its employees and the press.

While NASA worked to restore its communication systems, it also tried to uncover what had happened to Challenger. Senior managers associated with the launch gathered together. They watched video of the explosion. They were initially unable to detect what had gone wrong from the tapes.

Some people at NASA understood that they needed to communicate with the media immediately. They encouraged leaders at the agency to talk to the press. They wanted Associate Administrator of Space Flight Jesse Moore to give a press conference. They knew that the public was waiting. But Moore was not concerned with talking to the press. He was too busy trying to understand what had just happened. He prioritized organizing an investigation into the accident over speaking with the media.

In the absence of information from NASA, the U.S. news media tried to come up with their own explanations. Several journalists speculated about whether the icy conditions had contributed to the explosion. Some suggested there could be other causes. CBS news correspondent Bruce Hall wondered if something had gone wrong with the launch. He said, "It appeared to be one of the slowest liftoffs that any of us have seen." Without more information to share with their viewers, newscasters such as Tom Brokaw and Dan Rather simply reviewed what they did know. They showed their audiences small models of the space shuttle. They used these to explain the spacecraft's different parts. They also repeatedly showed footage of the explosion.

About 20 minutes after the explosion, news stations interrupted their broadcasts to show White House press secretary Larry Speakes giving a briefing. Speakes said that President Reagan was saddened by the event. He also noted that the president was anxious to have more information. He said the White House was getting its information about the incident from "what is being provided to the public on television." These statements highlighted the fact that the nation was waiting for details from NASA.

It took five hours before NASA was ready to give a statement to the press. This long delay allowed many journalists to travel to Florida to attend the conference in person. In fact, so many media people came to the press conference that it had to be moved to an outdoor grandstand to accommodate their large number.

Jesse Moore was the first NASA official to address the Challenger disaster.

Television news outlets aired the press conference. NASA administrator Moore took a seat at a desk in front of a crowd of journalists. He wore a dark blue trench coat over his suit—evidence of the still chilly Florida temperatures. Behind him was the sprawling Kennedy Space Center complex. Moore began, "It is with deep, heartfelt sorrow that I address you here this afternoon. At 11:40 a.m. this morning, the space program experienced a national tragedy with the explosion of the space shuttle Challenger. . . . I regret that I have to report that, based on very preliminary searches of the ocean where the Challenger impacted this morning, these searches have not revealed any evidence that the crew of Challenger survived."

Moore said that NASA was going to suspend all future flights until they could understand what had happened to Challenger. He said, "We're obviously not going to pick up any flight activity until we fully understand what the circumstances were."

As the day wore on, television newscasters would share this question with much of the nation: What, exactly, had happened to Challenger? News anchors stayed at their desks for hours, their on-air coverage stretching into evening news programs and beyond. ABC and NBC spent their entire evening news programs discussing the disaster. CBS featured other stories as well as the Challenger event.

At 5:00 p.m. President Reagan gave a statement. Many television news and radio stations interrupted their broadcasts to feature it live. Reagan had been scheduled to deliver his State of the Union speech that day. However, in light of the tragedy, he had rescheduled it for the following week. Instead of discussing the state of the country, Reagan found himself addressing a nation about grief, fear, and uncertainty.

Reagan said that he and first lady Nancy Reagan were "pained to the core by the tragedy of the shuttle Challenger." He called the crew heroes and pioneers.

And then he addressed the schoolchildren who had watched the disaster live in their classrooms. He said, "I know it is hard to understand, but sometimes

President Reagan canceled his State of the Union speech to reach out to a grieving nation on the day of the Challenger explosion.

painful things like this happen. It's all part of the process of exploration and discovery. It's all part of taking a chance and expanding man's horizons. The future doesn't belong to the fainthearted; it belongs to the brave."

ChapterFour
AFTER THE EXPLOSION

In the immediate aftermath of the explosion, search boats could not approach the disaster area. It was too dangerous. Debris from the destroyed space shuttle fell from the sky for more than an hour. Rescue teams could be hurt if they were hit by any large pieces of metal. In a desperate attempt to find the crew, paramedics parachuted into the area. They searched the waters amid the falling scraps.

After most of the wreckage fell into the ocean, rescue boats and airplanes entered the area. They tried to find Challenger's crew. These efforts were futile. All they were able to find were small fragments of the destroyed shuttle. The search would stretch on for months.

In the meantime, NASA opened an internal investigation into the accident. Flight controllers and engineers looked through their computer data. They studied photos and videos of the launch and explosion. This investigation was troubled from the beginning. NASA is a very large organization. It has facilities spread across the country. It also contracts with various private companies. This meant that people at the agency sometimes struggled to find the information they needed for their investigation. Adding to this confusion was the unstable leadership at the time.

Part of
Challenger's
right wing was
found amid the
wreckage.

NASA's leader, Administrator James Beggs, was on a leave of absence when the disaster occurred. A less experienced person named William Graham was filling in for him at the time. NASA's work was so disorganized that it would later be called "organizational chaos" by a person involved in the investigation.

As it worked to uncover the cause of the disaster, NASA was very closed off from the media. NASA officials told the press that they did not want to answer any questions until they had completed their own investigation of the accident. This created an atmosphere of mistrust. Many people thought that NASA was hiding information.

This recovered piece of exterior tiling was transported to Cape Canaveral by a rescue team.

On February 1 NASA released a video showing flames coming from one of Challenger's solid rocket boosters. The NASA official who briefed the press on the footage would not use the word "flame." Instead, he called it an "anomalous plume." The following day, NBC correspondent Jay Barbree reported that there had been a rupture in the right solid rocket booster. NASA would not confirm this report. The agency's reluctance to comment on Barbree's report further raised suspicions that NASA was concealing something from the public.

NASA employees analyzed the tapes from the mission to try to understand what went wrong.

People were angry about NASA's response to the disaster. Many journalists began to doggedly pursue NASA employees. They wanted to know what was happening with the investigation. Some reporters followed NASA employees to their doorsteps at night. Others monitored ships as they sailed in and out of the disaster area. Reporters hoped to catch a glimpse of the pieces of the shuttle.

President Reagan also established a commission to investigate what had happened. It became known as the Rogers Commission, after William P. Rogers, the commission's chairman. It called upon experts such as astronauts Neil Armstrong and Sally Ride. Other engineers, pilots, physicists, and an astronomer helped as well.

In March 1986, the crew cabin of Challenger was found about 15 miles (24 km) from the launch site.

It was about 100 feet (30 m) underwater. The lifeless bodies of seven crew members were still inside the cabin. NASA did not tell the public about this discovery right away. The agency planned to tell the families about their loved ones first, and then explain it to the media. However, reporters learned of the discovery. They shared this information through the media. At least one family, that of Ronald McNair, learned from news reports that their loved one's body had been found.

NASA's decision to withhold information from the public about the crew may have been well-intentioned. Accident investigators learned some upsetting truths about what might have happened to Challenger's crew. It appeared that the explosion may not have killed the astronauts. Rather, they may have died when their intact cabin hit the ocean water. This happened about 2 minutes and 45 seconds after the explosion. NASA may have wanted to spare the astronauts' families from having this information become public.

However, the agency's reluctance to share its discoveries with the public contributed to the idea that it was deliberately withholding information. Many speculated that NASA was covering up mistakes.

On June 6, 1986, the Rogers Commission released a report of its findings. This report showed that NASA had made mistakes that caused the disaster. It noted that the official cause of the accident was the failure

The Rogers Commission conducted a thorough investigation of the explosion.

of the O-rings in the right solid rocket booster. However, the commission also found that NASA's decision to launch in such cold weather had contributed to the disaster. It highlighted communication problems within the agency and concluded "that there was a serious flaw in the decision-making process leading up to the launch of Flight 51-L."

The Rogers Commission also pointed to other problems within NASA. It noted that the agency was working too fast and without the right safety and oversight. It recommended new safety protocols for future flights. It also recommended that NASA change some abort procedures for shuttle flights. These might make it easier for future astronauts to survive launch malfunctions.

Television newscasters devoted air time to this new chapter of the Challenger story. On ABC, host Peter Jennings was joined by astronaut Gene Cernan as they discussed the Rogers Commission's findings. Cernan expressed concerns about the state of the space agency. He said, "today it appears. . . . It's appalling almost that people are unwilling to admit that maybe they might have made a poor decision." He also noted that some people within NASA felt "somewhat betrayed because there were decisions made that they know should not have been made." President Reagan also made a televised appearance when the commission's official report was released. He gave a speech in the White House Rose Garden in which he promised that the U.S. space program would continue. Reagan said, "We'll work twice as hard and be twice as vigilant."

NASA took the findings of the Rogers Commission very seriously. It suspended future shuttle flights for nearly three years while it worked to improve the

"It's appalling almost that people are unwilling to admit that maybe they might have made a poor decision."

safety of the shuttle. It also developed new procedures to minimize the chances that a disaster like this would happen again. NASA did not just adjust its technology. It also reworked the way people in the agency would communicate with one another. NASA wanted to be sure that any concerns could be quickly passed to the right people.

On September 29, 1988, NASA resumed its shuttle program with the launch of Discovery, mission STS-26. Unlike the doomed Challenger launch in 1986, this launch was aired live by many news outlets. This showed that Challenger had reminded people of the dangers of spaceflight. But it had also emphasized just how important the U.S. crewed space program was to the nation. Once again, Americans were interested in space. They were rooting for their astronauts. Fortunately, mission STS-26 was a success.

The Challenger disaster was also an iconic event in TV news history. In the moments following the disaster, news stations showed footage of the explosion over and over again. In a time before social media and multiple 24-hour news networks, seeing this repetitive broadcast was an unusual phenomenon.

One *Washington Post* writer noted that perhaps this represented the start of a new type of news coverage: "We may not be able to believe that something truly terrible has happened anymore unless we see it six or seven times on television."

In the decades since the Challenger tragedy, much has changed in both TV and U.S. spaceflight. Modern TV viewers are now accustomed to watching the same video clip several times in the same broadcast. What had once been a shocking and unfamiliar experience is now ordinary. In fact, it is such a common occurrence that some networks have tried to impose rules on not showing upsetting footage too many times. In the days after the 9/11 attacks, ABC News president David Westin limited the number of times his news network could show the second plane hitting the World Trade Center. He made this decision out of concern that the upsetting footage might make children watching TV think that additional attacks were occurring.

U.S. spaceflight has evolved significantly since the loss of Challenger. The last space shuttle mission launched on July 8, 2011. It was the 135th STS mission. NASA retired the shuttles in order to focus on new space projects. These include potential missions to the moon, Mars, and asteroids. NASA astronauts still fly in space. They do so in partnership with other countries' space agencies, such as Russia's Roscosmos.

On October 11, 2018, NASA TV's live feed showed a desolate landscape. At the center was a Russian Soyuz spacecraft atop a towering rocket. Inside were U.S. astronaut Nick Hague and Russian cosmonaut Alexey Ovchinin. They were about to head to the International Space Station.

THE COLUMBIA DISASTER

Kennedy Space Center employees created this memorial to the Columbia crew shortly after the disaster.

After the Challenger disaster, NASA was harshly criticized for withholding information from the public. Agency officials knew their behavior would have to be more transparent if another disaster ever occurred.

On January 16, 2003, the space shuttle Columbia launched for mission STS-107. As it lifted off, one of its wings was damaged. This damage made the orbiter unstable. Sixteen days later, as Columbia returned to Earth at the conclusion of its mission, disaster struck. The shuttle broke apart as it reentered Earth's atmosphere. All seven astronauts on board were killed. NASA's response was quick and public. It opened its public affairs offices immediately to the press. It also worked hard to update the public on all aspects of the disaster response. This included recovering parts of the destroyed shuttle, investigating the cause of the disaster, and memorializing the lost crew. In order to accomplish this, NASA staffed its media room with people around the clock. NASA also broadcast many aspects of its own investigation into the accident. The public appreciated this open response after the Columbia disaster. NASA's transparency made many Americans feel confident that the space agency was not hiding anything.

The launch of Expedition 57 went wrong about two minutes into the flight.

NASA's cameras captured the thrilling moment of launch when the huge rocket heaved skyward. Much as it had during the first moments of the Challenger mission, everything seemed normal. However, in a chilling echo of the events of 1986, something went wrong with the powerful rocket. The astronauts didn't know it yet, but they were in serious trouble. An automated safety system sensed the problem with the rocket. A warning light flashed inside their tiny cockpit and the space capsule's safety system initiated an emergency abort. Hague and Ovchinin felt a huge jolt as the safety system took over and blasted their capsule safely away from the malfunctioning rocket. The two men soared upward in an arcing path before beginning to descend back to Earth. When they were low enough, a set of parachutes deployed. These slowed their capsule enough so that it could land safely.

This near-disaster was a powerful reminder of the dangers of spaceflight and the importance of proper safety precautions. In the days after his failed launch, Hague's troubled mission was a hot news story on television. In an interview after the aborted mission, Hague said he was grateful for the engineers who designed the safety systems in his spacecraft. He said, "I'd much rather be [on the Space Station], but I'm super thankful that I'm alive and kicking today."

Timeline

October 1, 1958

The National Aeronautics and Space Administration (NASA) is officially created.

1961–1972

NASA launches its first crewed space missions on board Mercury, Gemini, and Apollo spacecrafts.

September 17, 1976

NASA unveils its first shuttle, Enterprise. Stars of the television show *Star Trek* are on site for the unveiling.

January 5, 1972

President Richard Nixon approves a bill that will fund the development of the space shuttle.

April 12, 1981

NASA's first fully operational space shuttle, Columbia, makes its first spaceflight.

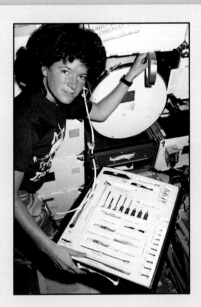

June 18, 1983

Sally Ride becomes the first American woman to fly in space on board Challenger, mission STS-7.

Timeline

August 30, 1983

Guion "Guy" Bluford Jr. becomes the first African American man to fly in space on board Challenger, mission STS-8.

July 19, 1985

Vice President George H.W. Bush announces that Christa McAuliffe will be the first Teacher in Space.

June 6, 1986

The Rogers Commission issues its report on the Challenger accident.

January 27, 1986

Engineers at Morton Thiokol issue a warning to NASA. The temperatures are too cold to safely launch Challenger.

January 28, 1986

The space shuttle Challenger, mission STS-51L, launches. At 73 seconds after launch, an explosion fatally compromises the orbiter. The crew is killed.

September 29, 1988

After a pause of nearly three years, NASA resumes shuttle flights with mission STS-26.

February 1, 2003

The space shuttle Columbia breaks apart as it returns to Earth after mission STS-107. The crew is killed.

Glossary

abort—to stop something right away because of a problem

astronomer—person who studies celestial objects, space, and the universe

buffeted—rocked violently by winds

contrail—a trail of condensed water vapor left behind by a spacecraft or aircraft

debris—loose or broken pieces

egalitarian—the idea that all people are equal and deserve equal opportunities and rights

Max Q—the period during a rocket launch when the launch vehicle is under the greatest stress; also known as Maximum Dynamic Pressure

NASA—National Aeronautics and Space Administration, which runs the U.S. space program

orbiter—the winged spaceplane component of the Space Transport System (STS)

plume—a long cloud of smoke or vapor resembling a feather

physicist—person who studies physics, the science of matter and energy

satellite—object in space that orbits another object, such as a planet; many satellites are human made

throttling—adding power to something

white room—the area astronauts use to do their final preparations for spaceflight

Additional Resources

Further Reading

Bodden, Valerie. *The Challenger Explosion.* Mankato, MN: Creative Paperbacks, 2018.

Braun, Eric. *Fatal Faults: The Story of the Challenger Disaster.* Mankato, MN: Capstone Press, 2015.

Kluger, Jeffrey. *Disaster Strikes! The Most Dangerous Space Missions of All Time.* New York: Philomel Books, 2019.

Internet Sites

NASA's Space Shuttle—From Top to Bottom
https://www.space.com/10727-nasa-space-shuttle-spacecraft.html

President Reagan's National Address on the Explosion of the Challenger
https://history.nasa.gov/reagan12886.html

The Space Shuttle Program
https://www.nasa.gov/audience/forstudents/k-4/stories/nasa-knows/what-is-the-space-shuttle-k4.html

Critical Thinking Questions

Consider the grainy quality of the video footage of the Challenger explosion. How do you think this contributed to the confusion that followed the accident?

Newscasters had little information for their viewers in the immediate aftermath of the accident. How did this affect the way they reported the news to their viewers?

The Challenger explosion was one of the first disasters to be played over and over on television news. How do you think this affected the way people thought about the incident?

Source Notes

p. 4, "Looks like we're going..." Jay Hamburg, "The Final Hours of Space Shuttle Challenger," *Orlando Sentinel*, January 28, 2006, https://www.orlandosentinel.com/news/space/orl-challenger-lastmoments-story.html Accessed December 1, 2018.

p. 7, "Save it for me..." Ibid.

p. 12, "Aaall riight!" Ibid.

p. 12, "Be quiet..." Troy Kent, "Memories of the Challenger Explosion from Our Readers," *Daytona Beach News-Journal*, August 15, 2011, https://www.news-journalonline.com/news/20110127/memories-of-the-challenger-explosion-from-our-readers Accessed January 20, 2019.

p. 12, "Thirty seconds down there..." "The Final Hours of Space Shuttle Challenger."

p. 13, "crucial role..." "Teachers in Space: The History," Citizens in Space, 2012, http://www.citizensinspace.org/teachers-in-space-the-history/ Accessed November 20, 2018.

p. 14, "There they go..." "The Final Hours of Space Shuttle Challenger."

p. 14, "All right!" "Ibid.

p. 14, "Here we go..." Ibid.

p. 14, "Looks like we've..." "Transcript of the Challenger Crew Comments from the Operational Recorder," NASA, 1986, https://history.nasa.gov/transcript.html Accessed January 20, 2019.

p. 14, "There's Mach 1..." Ibid.

p. 15, "One minute..." "The Final Hours of the Space Shuttle Challenger."

p. 16, "Uh oh..." Ibid.

p. 18, "Where's the shuttle?" Ibid.

p. 18, "Flight controllers..." "Ibid.

p. 30, "The ice has cleared..." "The Challenger Disaster CNN Live Coverage 11:00AM- 12:00PM January 28, 1986," YouTube, November 29, 2016, https://www.youtube.com/watch?v=fEwNMmhOVF4 Accessed November 20, 2018.

p. 30, "We have main engines..." Ibid.

p. 32, "Houston, Challenger..." Ibid.

p. 34, "I am appalled..." "Remembering Roger Boisjoly: He Tried to Stop Shuttle Challenger Launch," National Public Radio, February 26, 2012, https://www.npr.org/sections/thetwo-way/2012/02/06/146490064/remembering-roger-boisjoly-he-tried-to-stop-shuttle-challenger-launch Accessed February 26, 2019.

p. 34, "We made it!" Ibid.

p. 35, "So the 25th..." "The Challenger Disaster."

p. 35, "Looks like a couple..." Ibid.

p. 35, "total chaos..." William Harwood, "Reporters Recall Challenger Disaster 30 Years Later," CBS News, January 20, 2018, https://www.cbsnews.com/news/reporters-remember-challenger-disaster-30-years-later/ Accessed November 20, 2018.

p. 37, "Shut up in here!" "1986: Space Shuttle Challenger Explosion," CNN, https://www.cnn.com/videos/us/2013/06/03/vault-backstory-1986-challenger-disaster.cnn/video/playlists/atv-moments-in-history/ Accessed November 20, 2018.

p. 37, "This story is..." "CBS News Live Coverage of the Challenger Disaster Part 1," YouTube, January 19, 2010, https://www.youtube.com/watch?v=DdETXRvFaew Accessed November 20, 2018.

p. 38, "What you have..." Ibid.

p. 40, "It appeared to be..." "The Challenger Disaster: CBS News Special Report." YouTube, August 30, 2016, https://www.youtube.com/watch?v=_2MNAaQHeLw&t=1187s Accessed November 20, 2018.

p. 42, "I regret..." Jesse Moore, "Transcript of NASA News Conference on the Shuttle Disaster," *New York Times*, January 29, 1986, https://www.nytimes.com/1986/01/29/us/the-shuttle-explosion-transcript-of-nasa-news-conference-on-the-shuttle-disaster.html Accessed January 21, 2019.

p. 42, "We're obviously..." Ibid.

p. 42, "pained to the core..." Ronald W. Reagan, "Explosion of the Space Shuttle Challenger: Address to the Nation, January 28, 1986," NASA, https://history.nasa.gov/reagan12886.html Accessed December 10, 2018.

pp. 42–43, "I know it is hard..." Ibid.

p. 45, "Organizational chaos..." Dianne Vaughan. *The Challenger Launch Decision: Risky Technology, Culture, and Deviance at NASA*. Chicago: University of Chicago Press, 1996, p. 54.

p. 46, "anomalous plume..." "Reporters Recall Challenger Disaster 30 Years Later."

p. 50, "today it appears..." "ABC June 1986 Coverage of Rogers Commission Findings." YouTube, February 10, 2014, https://www.youtube.com/watch?v=KG7nKU3wNF0 Accessed November 20, 2018.

p. 50, "We'll work twice as hard..." "Ibid.

p. 51, "We may not be able..." Dan Zak, "'We've Lost 'Em, God Bless 'Em': What It Was Like to Witness the Challenger Explode," *The Hamilton Spectator*, January 28, 2016, https://www.thespec.com/news-story/6253141--we-ve-lost-em-god-bless-em-what-it-was-like-to-witness-the-challenger-explode/ Accessed November 20, 2018.

p. 55, "I'd much rather be..." Eric Niiler, "Here's What Astronauts See When a Rocket Aborts Mid-Flight," *Wired*, October 16, 2018, https://www.wired.com/story/heres-what-astronauts-see-when-a-rocket-aborts-mid-flight/ Accessed January 20, 2019.

Select Bibliography

Books

Harris, Hugh. *Challenger: An American Tragedy: The Inside Story from Launch Control.* New York: Open Road Media, 2014.

Websites and Articles

"1986: Space Shuttle Challenger Explosion," CNN, https://www.cnn.com/videos/us/2013/06/03/vault-backstory-1986-challenger-disaster.cnn/video/playlists/atv-moments-in-history/ Accessed November 20, 2018.

"ABC June 1986 Coverage of Rogers Commission Findings," YouTube, February 10, 2014, https://www.youtube.com/watch?v=KG7nKU3wNF0 Accessed November 20, 2018.

Berkes, Howard, "Remembering Roger Boisjoly: He Tried to Stop Shuttle Challenger's Launch," National Public Radio, February 6, 2012, https://www.npr.org/sections/thetwo-way/2012/02/06/146490064/remembering-roger-boisjoly-he-tried-to-stop-shuttle-challenger-launch Accessed November 20, 2018.

"CBS News Live Coverage of the Challenger Disaster Part 1," YouTube, January 19, 2010, https://www.youtube.com/watch?v=DdETXRvFaew Accessed November 20, 2018.

"The Challenger Disaster: CBS News Special Report," YouTube, August 30, 2016, https://www.youtube.com/watch?v=_2MNAaQHeLw&t=1187s Accessed November 20, 2018.

"The Challenger Disaster CNN Live Coverage 11:00AM–12:00PM January 28, 1986," YouTube, November 29, 2016, https://www.youtube.com/watch?v=fEwNMmhOVF4 Accessed November 20, 2018.

"Changes in Shuttle Post Challenger and Columbia," NASA, December 1, 2018, https://ntrs.nasa.gov/archive/nasa/casi.ntrs.nasa.gov/20100030545.pdf Accessed January 20, 2019.

Fisher, Marc, and Ellen Livingston. "Space Shuttle Challenger Exploded 30 Years Ago Over Florida with Teacher on Board," *Miami Herald*, January 26, 2018, https://www.miamiherald.com/news/state/florida/article56593163.html Accessed December 10, 2018.

Hamburg, Jay. "The Final Hours of the Challenger Space Shuttle," *Orlando Sentinel*, January 28, 2006, https://www.orlandosentinel.com/news/space/orl-challenger-lastmoments-story.html Accessed December 1, 2018.

Harwood, William, "Reporters Recall Challenger Disaster 30 Years Later," CBS News, January 27, 2018, https://www.cbsnews.com/news/reporters-remember-challenger-disaster-30-years-later/ Accessed November 20, 2018.

Hohler, Robert, "Teacher Passes her NASA Tests with Flying Colors," *Los Angeles Times*, January 26, 1987, http://articles.latimes.com/1987-01-26/news/vw-889_1_test-lab/2 Accessed November 20, 2018.

Holston, Noel, "Coverage from the Day the Challenger Exploded..." *Orlando Sentinel*, January 29, 1986, https://www.orlandosentinel.com/business/space/orl-challenger-25-day-of-tv-reaction-story.html Accessed November 20, 2018.

Howell, Elizabeth, "Guion Bluford: First African-American in Space," Space.com, February 8, 2018, https://www.space.com/25602-guion-bluford-biography.html Accessed December 1, 2018.

"John Glenn's Earth Orbit Diary from the Friendship 7 in 1962," *Newsweek*, February 20, 2017, https://www.newsweek.com/john-glenn-friendship-7-orbit-earth-diary-558527 Accessed November 20, 2018.

"Nixon Launches the Space Shuttle Program," History, August 21, 2018, https://www.history.com/this-day-in-history/nixon-launches-the-space-shuttle-program Accessed December 10, 2018.

Reagan, Ronald W., "Explosion of the Space Shuttle Challenger: Address to the Nation, January 28, 1986," NASA, https://history.nasa.gov/reagan12886.html Accessed November 20, 2018.

Rensenberger, Boyce, and Kathy Sawyer, "Challenger Disaster Blamed on O-Rings, Presure to Launch," *Washington Post*, June 10, 1986, https://www.washingtonpost.com/archive/politics/1986/06/10/challenger-disaster-blamed-on-o-rings-pressure-to-launch/6b331ca1-f544-4147-8e4e-941b7a7e47ae/?utm_term=.d22c900eea09 Accessed November 20, 2018.

Rogers, William P., et al., "Report to the President by the Presidential Commission on the Space Shuttle Challenger Accident," June 6, 1982, https://spaceflight.nasa.gov/outreach/SignificantIncidents/assets/rogers_commission_report.pdf Accessed November 20, 2018.

"The Shuttle Findings: A Long Series of Failures...," *New York Times*, June 10, 1986, https://www.nytimes.com/1986/06/10/science/shuttle-findings-long-series-failures-key-portions-commission-report-challenger.html Accessed November 20, 2018.

"The Space Shuttle Is Dead, Long Live the Space Shuttle!" National Public Radio, July 15, 2011, https://www.npr.org/2011/07/15/137857866/the-space-shuttle-is-dead-long-live-the-space-shuttle Accessed December 10, 2018.

"Star Trek and NASA: 50 Years of Fictional and Factual Space History Crossovers," collectSPACE, http://www.collectspace.com/news/news-090816a-star-trek-50-nasa-crossovers.html Accessed November 20, 2018.

Sullivan, Ronald, "Some Wept, Some Slept, and Some Saw Liftoff as a Big Waste of Money," *New York Times*, April 13,1981, https://archive.nytimes.com/www.nytimes.com/library/national/science/041381sci-nasa-columbia-5.html Accessed November 20, 2018.

"Teachers in Space: The History," Citizens In Space, 2012, http://www.citizensinspace.org/teachers-in-space-the-history/ Accessed November 20, 2018.

"Transcript of the Challenger Crew Comments from the Operational Recorder," NASA, https://history.nasa.gov/transcript.html Accessed November 20, 2018.

Zak, Dan, "'We've Lost 'Em, God Bless 'Em': What It was Like to Witness the Challenger Explode," *The Hamilton Spectator*, January 28, 2016, https://www.thespec.com/news-story/6253141--we-ve-lost-em-god-bless-em-what-it-was-like-to-witness-the-challenger-explode/ Accessed November 20, 2018.

Index

About the Author

The Challenger holds a special place in author Rebecca Rissman's heart. On the frigid morning of January 28, 1986, she watched the launch along with her mother and sisters in a Florida parking lot. Today, Rissman is an accomplished nonfiction author. She has written more than 300 books about art, history, science, and culture. But her favorite topic to write about is the same one that pulled her into that cold, blustery parking lot all those years ago: spaceflight.

PER ASPERA AD ASTRA.

A rough road leads to the stars.